CONFRONTING
SEXISM

LAURA LA BELLA

Rosen
YA

New York

Published in 2018 by The Rosen Publishing Group, Inc.
29 East 21st Street, New York, NY 10010

Library of Congress Cataloging-in-Publication Data

Names: La Bella, Laura, author.
Title: Confronting sexism / Laura La Bella.
Description: New York: Rosen Publishing, 2018 | Series: Speak up! Confronting discrimination in your daily life | Includes bibliographical references and index.
Identifiers: LCCN 2017023287| ISBN 9781538381823 (library bound) | ISBN 9781538381809 (pbk.) | ISBN 9781538381816 (6 pack)
Subjects: LCSH: Sexism—Juvenile literature.
Classification: LCC HQ1237 .L33 2018 | DDC 305.3—dc23
LC record available at https://lccn.loc.gov/2017023287

Manufactured in China

CONTENTS

INTRODUCTION

I n March 2014, administrators at Haven Middle School in Evanston, Illinois, sent a memo home notifying parents that female students were banned from wearing shorts, leggings, and yoga pants. These items of clothing were deemed too distracting to male students.

The memo ignited protests and outcries from female students and their parents. In a letter to school administrators, one student's mother wrote, "This policy clearly shifts the blame for boys' behavior or lack of academic concentration directly onto the girls … This kind of message lands itself squarely on a continuum that blames girls and women for assault by men. It also sends the message to boys that their behaviors are excusable or understandable given what the girls are wearing."

Many parents and students reasoned that instead of asking girls to modify their wardrobe choices, school administrators should focus on teaching boys to stop objectifying young women and educate them on the potential harms of sexist behavior. As one female student said, "Not being able to wear leggings because it's 'too distracting for boys' is giving us the impression we should be guilty for what guys do."

Haven Middle School isn't alone in singling out female students and blaming them for the behaviors and attitudes of male students; schools in California, Minnesota, and Vermont have also banned shorts,

A student wrote the hashtag #iamnotadistraction on her arm as part of her protest against the dress code policy at her school, which has directed female students to wear what the district has defined as "more modest" clothing choices.

leggings, tank tops, and other clothing for similar reasons. The idea that women and girls must modify what they wear, say, or do to avoid distracting, drawing the attention of, or enabling men and young boys to act in inappropriate ways is an example of sexism—the idea and belief that one gender is superior to another. Sexism includes the attitudes, beliefs, stereotypes, and biases that promote the idea that women are worth less than men. And everywhere we turn, sexism is present.

On the red carpet, actresses are asked what designer they are wearing, while actors are asked what motivated them to take a particular role. In schools, boys are given preference in science and math courses. According to *Time* magazine, two studies on gender bias in education found that teachers spend up to two-thirds of their time talking to male students and that teachers are more likely to interrupt girls in class. In video games and comic books, women have historically been illustrated with unrealistic figures wearing minimal clothing while

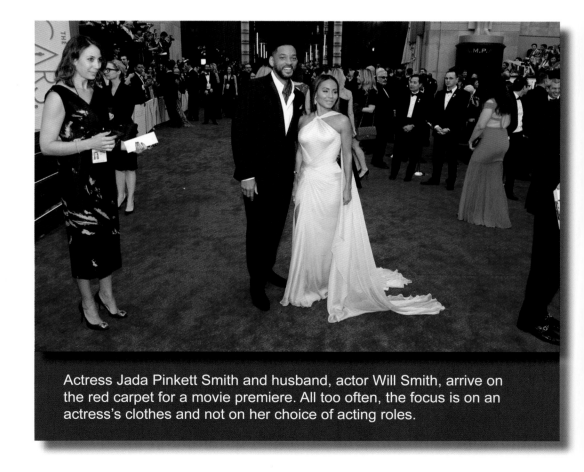

Actress Jada Pinkett Smith and husband, actor Will Smith, arrive on the red carpet for a movie premiere. All too often, the focus is on an actress's clothes and not on her choice of acting roles.

male characters are drawn to be strong and athletic. In home and work environments, women who speak up or voice concerns are defined as bossy or hysterical.

These comments and attitudes feed into sexism, impacting how women feel about themselves. Sexism inherently demeans women's contributions—to their schools, workplaces, and communities—and can make them feel depressed, angry, or anxious. They also undermine gender equality—or, encouragement of equal treatment, rights, status, and opportunities for all people—which has an effect on society as a whole.

Combating sexism begins by learning what sexism is, how to recognize and confront sexist situations, and where to turn to get help if you find yourself at the receiving end of it.

CHAPTER ONE

WHAT IS SEXISM?

S usan J. Fowler joined the transportation company Uber in 2015. After her initial training, she chose to work on a team where she could use her expertise in reliability engineering, an area that focuses on the dependability of a product. Once she began work, Fowler started receiving chat messages from her team manager requesting that she engage in an inappropriate relationship with him. Fowler saved the messages and reported him to human resources.

A company's human resource (HR) department oversees different aspects of employment, such as health benefits, recruitment, and dismissal. It's also the department an employee turns to when something inappropriate occurs on the job, from sexual harassment to racial discrimination. An HR employee at Uber informed Fowler that her manager was a high performer for the company and this was his first offense. Uber would give him no more than a warning. They also gave Fowler an option: she could stay on this man's team and expect a poor performance review from him in the future—which they told her they could do nothing about—or she could find another team to work with in an attempt to avoid working with him. Fowler chose to leave the team.

Uber, the ride-sharing company, found itself in the news again in June 2017 when a top executive of the company tried to use a woman's confidential medical history to discredit her claims of rape.

Over the next few months, Fowler met other female employees and learned that this man had behaved the same way with them. With each complaint these women made to human resources, the response was exactly the same. Each was told it was the man's first offense. Fowler and a group of women all went to human resources to demand that something be done about the man's behavior. In private meetings, each woman was told that no one else had complained about him and that no further action would be taken.

Fowler continued to encounter sexism at Uber and was even threatened with termination for reporting these instances to human resources. She eventually left the company to pursue other opportunities. Fowler wrote about her experience online. The post caught the attention of Uber's CEO, Travis Kalanick, who ordered an investigation into his company's practices. Kalanick told Tech.Mic.com, "There can be absolutely no place for this kind of [sexist] behavior at Uber—and anyone who behaves this way or thinks this is OK will be fired."

FIGHTING FOR EQUALITY

The fight for equality between men and women in the United States dates back to the country's first gathering devoted to women's rights. Held July 19–20, 1848, in Seneca Falls, New York, this meeting launched a movement to give women equality in American society. The first item they tackled was the right to vote.

Ever since, women have been fighting for equality, with big gains and losses along the way, but it wasn't until the second women's rights movement in the 1960s that feminism and gender equality came to the forefront of American society. Evolving gender roles in the workplace empowered women to demand equality, including equal pay and maternity leave.

Modern-day sexism is tied to feminism, or the advocacy or support of women's rights based on the idea that men and women are equal. The term "sexism" emerged from a second wave of feminism that lasted from the 1960s through the '80s.

Until the 1960s, a woman in the United States was expected to follow one path: marry in her early twenties, start a family, and spend her life maintaining a home and raising children. Women were subjected to head and

The 1970 Women's Liberation demonstration in Washington, DC, celebrated the fiftieth anniversary of the passing of the Nineteenth Amendment, which gave women the right to vote. The strike also aimed to raise awareness for social and workforce equality and political rights for women.

master laws, which made their husbands the head of the home and the primary decision maker. A woman had no legal right to any of her husband's earnings or property, even though the husband could control his wife's property and any income earned outside the home. It was also difficult for a woman to get a divorce; wives had to prove wrongdoing by their husbands for a divorce to be granted.

According to a Bureau of Labor Statistics' report, "100 Years of Consumer Spending," in 1960, only 38 percent of American women worked, and their professions were largely limited to teaching, nursing,

Betty Friedan, author of *The Feminine Mystique*, also served as president of the National Organization for Women (NOW).

and secretarial roles. Women accounted for 6 percent of American doctors, 3 percent of lawyers, and less than 1 percent of engineers. Those women who did work were paid lower salaries than men and denied opportunities to advance.

One book began to change the tide for women. In 1962, Betty Friedan wrote *The Feminine Mystique*, a book that captured the frustration and despair of a generation of college-educated women who felt trapped and unfulfilled in their daily lives as housewives and mothers. Friedan's book is credited with sparking the second wave of feminism, which empowered women to demand workplace equality, access to better jobs, and equal pay through the creation of antidiscrimination laws.

SEXISM, MISOGYNY, AND CHAUVINISM: WHAT ARE THE DIFFERENCES?

When a group of people only listens to suggestions made by a man, this is sexism. When a group of people only listens to suggestions made by a man and they belittle, mock, and criticize a woman when she makes the same suggestions, this is misogyny. When a man orders food for a woman without asking her what she'd prefer to eat, or controls other aspects of her life such as her clothing choices or her friends, this is chauvinism.

(continued on the next page)

(continued from the previous page)

Sexism is an attitude or belief that women are lesser than men. In the classroom, this happens when male students are called upon more frequently than female students, or when a male student is allowed to interrupt a female student while she's speaking.

Misogyny is an ingrained hatred or deeply rooted dislike for women and girls. Misogynistic attitudes or behaviors include intimidating or humiliating women, trying to destroy their self-esteem and confidence, objectifying women, being violent toward women, and being possessive of a woman's time and energy. Sexual discrimination and sexual assault often fall into this category.

Chauvinism is used to describe men who strongly believe in the superiority of their own gender. Chauvinists often think of women as incapable of making their own decisions. They are often controlling in their behavior. They might tell a girl or a woman what to wear, where to go, or what she can and cannot do.

Attitudes and behaviors toward women span a wide range in the United States, from naïve assumptions to sexual violence; clarifying confusion around these terms helps people understand the motivations and attitudes behind how they and others are being treated.

In 1964, Representative Howard Smith of Virginia added a prohibition on gender discrimination into the Civil Rights Act that was then under consideration. The Civil Rights Act of 1964 was a landmark amendment to the US Constitution. The act made it unlawful to discriminate against workers based on race, color, religion, gender, or national origin.

TYPES OF SEXISM

Sexism and sexist attitudes serve to support the idea that men are dominant over women. This is called patriarchy, or male dominance. In this type of society, men are predominately given positions of power while women are excluded from top leadership roles.

There are two main types of sexism: hostile and benevolent. Hostile sexism is an antagonistic or aggressive attitude toward women. The actions of a hostile sexist come from men who think that women are incompetent and inferior to men. Behaviors that are threatening, intimidating, or abusive to women are examples of hostile sexism. Some examples of behaviors associated with hostile sexism include:

- Touching or fondling women inappropriately;
- Controlling what women wear, where they go, and with whom they interact; and
- Treating women as property or possessions.

Benevolent sexism refers to actions or comments that may appear positive or harmless, but are actually damaging to women and serve to deny gender equality. Men who make benevolent sexist comments often see women as needing to be protected by men. Some examples of behaviors associated with benevolent sexism include:

- Dating only beautiful women, or encouraging a woman to actively improve her appearance rather than her mind;
- Asking a woman to make coffee or plan the company party when those tasks are unrelated to her job;

- Calling a woman "honey" or "sweetheart" rather than using more respectful language, such as her first name, outside of a consensual, romantic relationship; and
- Using the word "girl" when referring to an adult woman.

Hostile and benevolent sexism occur on three different levels. To overcome sexism, it is important to understand each level and its impact on women and society.

Institutionalized sexism occurs when sexism is integrated into our political, social, and economic institutions. Examples include laws that limit women's rights; media and entertainment that portray women as objects rather than intellectual, contributing members of society; and companies that pay women less than men for doing the same job.

Interpersonal sexism focuses on personal interactions with people who stereotype women as being inferior to men. This type of sexism includes the view that women should have fewer rights than others and that women are not capable of making their own decisions without input or approval from a man. Sexual harassment is an example of interpersonal sexism, as is treating women as sex objects.

Internalized sexism is when an individual has sexist attitudes toward herself and people of her own sex. Some examples of internalized sexism are when women believe they are inferior to men, that they do not believe they deserve to be treated equally, or when they judge each other based on appearance or behavior.

CHAPTER TWO

RECOGNIZING SEXISM

E leventh grade students at Highland High School in Salt Lake City, Utah, were given a homework assignment that asked them to go on a date that cost five dollars. The homework assignment, which was for students enrolled in an Adult Roles and Financial Literacy class, provided each gender with a handout outlining suggestions for appropriate behavior. The boys' list included recommendations from the girls such as "no gross noises," "chew with your mouth closed," and "it's okay to show your feelings." The girls' list of suggestions from boys—which was printed on pink paper—included suggestions such as "dress appropriately," "be feminine and lady-like," and "if you think you're too fat, keep it to yourself."

A HARMFUL ASSIGNMENT

First of all, requiring students to go out on real dates as a graded homework assignment for any class is absurd and inappropriate. Discussion of appropriate dating behavior in a classroom setting can be positive if approached correctly, as consent for any level of physical

In today's schools, encountering sexist attitudes is a common experience for girls. Research by two Northern Illinois University professors found that teachers attribute boys' skills in science to innate ability, while they see girls' abilities as a result of hard work.

interaction—from kissing to sexual activity—is a growing concern amid high school and college-aged students. Unfortunately, teaching dating behavior by enforcing stereotypical gender roles is not only irresponsible, it promotes sexist ideas that men and women are expected to act and behave according to different rules.

The assignment was gender biased, which is a form of prejudice and discrimination. By forcing students to go out on a date with someone of the opposite sex, it was also disrespectful to students who identify as lesbian, gay, bisexual, or transgender. And for some students who are either religious or just not interested, being required to date for a grade isn't OK.

This type of class assignment might be seen as funny or even enjoyable by some students, but the bottom line is it's a blatant form of sexism. Sometimes, as in this example, sexist comments are obvious. Other times they can be so subtle they are missed entirely. But many forms of sexist behavior, comments, and beliefs are ingrained in our society and even accepted as normal.

COMMON FORMS OF SEXISM

Before you can speak up about sexism in your life, it is important to be able to recognize it in some of its most common forms:

Everyday sexism—This basic form of sexism is experienced by women on a day-to-day basis. It can include overtly inappropriate comments as well as double standards, commonly used sexist language, offensive song lyrics, and sexist attitudes in school classrooms.

Religious sexism—In the Catholic faith, women are barred from becoming priests and even from participating in certain portions of religious ceremonies. In many

A sharia police officer questions a woman about her jeans in northern Sumatra, in Indonesia, in May 2016. Sexism is prevalent in the world's major religions, where women have historically been the objects of religious beliefs and practices that promote the rights of men over women.

religions, including Christianity, Judaism, and Islam, religious texts, spiritual leaders, religious experiences, and ceremonial rituals are focused on men.

Double standards—A double standard is when a rule or attitude is unfairly applied in different ways to different people or groups. Women who are promiscuous are "sluts," while men who engage in sexual activity are "studs" or seen as heroes. A hardworking, ambitious woman is seen as abrasive, difficult, or demanding while an equally ambitious man is referred to as driven, a good leader, and motivated. It's more generally acceptable for an older man to date a younger woman than for an older woman to date a younger man.

Slut shaming—Slut shaming is the practice of punishing women and girls for their real or assumed sexual behavior. These assumptions are often based on what a girl is wearing, how she is acting, what she looks like, and/or what sexual activities she does or does not participate in. Slut shaming is inclusive of blame or judgment toward women who have been raped or sexually assaulted.

Men and boys are not subjected to slut shaming. A man or teenage boy who has had sex or has had multiple sexual partners is not expected to feel shame, nor are they generally referred to as a "slut." Slut shaming challenges gender equality and encourages society to judge the normal sexual desires or behaviors of women and young girls in a negative way.

Slut shaming is incredibly dangerous, because it creates an environment that puts the responsibility for the actions of men and boys onto women. This kind of sexism enables rape apologists—people who blame rape victims for the assault based on their appearance, age, attitudes, and behavior. Yet again, it encourages

Model and TV personality Amber Rose hosts the annual Amber Rose SlutWalk Festival, a zero-tolerance event that celebrates women and raises awareness of the negative impact of hateful language, racism, sexism, ableism, fat shaming, transphobia, and other forms of bigotry.

the idea that men are unable to control themselves, and that women are responsible for keeping them in check.

AND WHERE TO FIND IT

It was the most popular song of 2013. "Blurred Lines" by Robin Thicke peaked at number one in twenty-five countries, sold 14.8 million copies worldwide, and was the longest running number one hit in the United States. It's also a song that's fraught with controversy over its lyrics. The song is about convincing a good girl that she wants to have sex—that she isn't asking for. With lines such as "I know you want it," "I hate these blurred lines," "That man is not your mate and that's why I'm gon' take you," the song—not to mention the music video—treats women as objects.

Degrading music lyrics—Sexist songs that objectify women can encourage the belief that women are not equal to men, permit the idea that it's okay to reduce women to objects, and can even promote a more tolerant attitude toward sexual assault or sexual violence. A study by researchers Cougar Hall, Joshua H. West, and Shane Hill from Brigham Young University determined that songs about sex can "lead young girls to judge their personal worth on a sexual level only, leading to poor body image, depression, eating disorders, and substance abuse."

Language—Our choice of words in describing gender can be sexist. Consider the following descriptions of men and women in leadership roles: "He's commanding, she's demanding." "He's assertive, she's aggressive." "He strategizes, she manipulates." In each of these examples the words used to describe men are all positive, leadership-based words that show respect for a man's aptitude and abilities. In contrast, the words used to describe women are negative and show contempt for a woman's knowledge and capacity in the workplace.

Sexist educational lessons—Studies have found that the US educational system promotes the contributions of men in society over female contributions. Students learn about Albert Einstein's impact in the field of science, but rarely the influence of female scientists. Even Nobel Prize winner Marie Curie is rarely mentioned separately from her husband and fellow scientist, Pierre. The educational system has failed to provide an accurate portrayal of women and their contributions to nearly all areas of study—a change we must demand and work toward achieving in our future.

When female students see successful women in a career field they wish to pursue, they feel like part of that community. This is key to getting female students to remain in fields that have been traditionally male dominated, such as engineering, the sciences, and math. According to an interview with Nilanjana Dasgupta, a psychology researcher at the University of Massachusetts, Amherst, low academic performance is not the primary reason why high school and college-aged women leave classes in science, technology,

Scientist Marie Curie is the first woman to win a Nobel Prize and the only person to win the award in two different fields, physics and chemistry.

engineering, and math (STEM). "Usually, women who leave STEM perform just as well as others who stay. Feeling like they fit in, or not, is the critical ingredient that determines retention," Dasgupta said in an article from the National Science Foundation. Feeling excluded, she added, makes students search for more inclusive academic environments, which leads students to drop or avoid certain types of classes.

MYTHS AND FACTS

MYTH
When a girl or woman wears short skirts or tight clothing, she's asking for sexual attention.

Fact
Women have the right to wear whatever clothing they want and should not be judged by their wardrobe decisions. According to the organization Rape Crisis, "People, and especially women and girls, of all ages, classes, culture, ability, sexuality, race, and faith are raped. The perceived 'attractiveness' of a victim has very little to do with sexual violence. Rape is an act of violence, not sex."

MYTH
Feminists hate men.

Fact
Feminism is about equality for men and women. It is not an anti-male movement nor is it designed to create hatred or animosity toward men and boys. Men can be feminists.

MYTH
Women are their own worst enemy.

Fact
This belief centers on the idea that because women can be mean to one another, society shouldn't afford them equality until all women get along. This deflects attention away from the problem of inequality and onto women themselves, stereotyping the entire female gender as a problem.

CHAPTER THREE

CLASSIFYING SEXISM

"SEND NOODZ," said the text message. "Wait what???" the girl responded. In her book, *American Girls: Social Media and the Secret Lives of Teenagers*, Nancy Jo Sales writes about what it's like for teenage girls to live in the digital age when social media and sexism collide.

For teenage girls, sexism occurs just as much online as it does in classrooms or in interactions with the opposite sex. Girls are being asked to text naked images of themselves. They encounter sexist behavior on social media and in person where they are slut shamed for their clothing choices, suspected sexual behavior, or even their friends. Social media may be a new place where sexism can occur, but girls and women have been facing sexism and sexist attitudes for generations. Confronting sexism in all its forms begins with understanding gender stereotypes and how attitudes about men and women are formed.

GENDER STEREOTYPES

Men are good at fixing cars. Women are better at cleaning the house. Neither of these statements is always true, but both illustrate typical gender

Smartphones have given rise to a number of inappropriate and dangerous behaviors, such as sexting, texting and driving, cyberbullying, and sharing too much personal information.

stereotypes surrounding the abilities and interests of boys and girls.

Stereotypes are generalizations made about groups of people based on widely accepted biases about features or traits that apply to a specific gender, ethnicity, nationality, race, or sexual orientation. Stereotypes can be both positive and negative but are rarely an accurate way of defining an entire group of people. Gender stereotypes occur when assumptions are made about all men or all women—from what they like to how they act. Stereotypically female behavior would include cooking, sewing, dancing, teaching, and caring for children, whereas some stereotypically male behavior includes camping, fishing, hiking, working on cars, and playing video games.

Gender stereotypes stem from beliefs and attitudes about masculinity and a man's role in society. They date back hundreds of years. And because of this long history, they are difficult to change. But by confronting sexism, society can begin to influence how women and girls are perceived and begin to create more equality between the sexes.

IS CHIVALRY A FORM OF SEXISM?

A young man stands up from his seat on a train and offers it to a woman. A businessman holds a door open to a female colleague. Are these examples of good manners or sexist behavior?

While hostile sexism is easier to spot, benevolent sexism is much harder and is sometimes considered part of our social manners. While some behaviors are seen as generous or even romantic—the man pays on the first date, the man proposes marriage—they may be indicative of ingrained expectations that women need to be treated differently than men. Would the same businessman who opened that door for his colleague have held the door for another man? If his answer is no, chances are high that he feels an ingrained need to be protective of women. Chivalry has historically been defined as a core

Chivalry conceals itself as courtesy. In reality, it creates an unequal atmosphere where women are viewed as fragile individuals in need of special protection and assistance.

(continued on the next page)

(continued from the previous page)

characteristic of masculinity. But if a man believes his wife won't be able to carry the groceries into the house on her own, will he also view a female manager as unfit to lead a corporation?

Instead of teaching boys to be gentlemen and girls to be ladies, young adults should be taught to be civil and kind *human beings* who are supportive and compassionate to everyone.

WOMEN CAN BE SEXIST, TOO

Sexism and sexist comments and attitudes are not just perpetuated by men. Women also make sexist statements and can have sexist beliefs.

Kellyanne Conway, special counsel to President Donald J. Trump, said: "If we were physiologically—not mentally, emotionally, professionally—equal to men, if we were physiologically as strong as men, rape would not exist ... You would be able to defend yourself and fight him off."

Conway's comment, which defines sexual assault victims as physically weak, implies that victims are responsible for their own rape. Her comment avoids certain facts about rape and sexual assault. First, not all sexual assaults are physically forceful; some occur when the victim is unconscious or under the influence of drugs or alcohol. Second, some rape victims are mentally or physically impaired because of a disability and do not have the capacity to defend themselves in any situation.

Campbell Brown, a former CNN news anchor, found herself on the receiving end of negative comments from a woman who focused more on Brown's appearance than on the substance of Brown's commentary.

Third, not all sexual assault victims are female. Men are also victims of rape.

Educational historian and advocate Diane Ravitch said the following about CNN journalist Campbell Brown: "She is a good media figure because of her looks, but she doesn't seem to know or understand anything about teaching and why tenure matters ... I know it sounds sexist to say that she is pretty, but that makes her telegenic, even if what she has to say is total nonsense."

Ravitch's comments demean Brown's knowledge of the subject matter by turning the focus of the conversation to Brown's appearance, which has no impact on intellectual capacity. Ravitch disagreed with Brown's comments, but chose to focus on Brown's appearance to discredit her rather than providing a fact-based counterargument to her statements.

CAN MEN EXPERIENCE SEXISM?

Men are strong and masculine. They like sports and are athletic. They are expected to be successful, financially supportive of their wives and children, and protective toward women. How many times have we heard these statements?

In the same way that it is sexist to expect women to be ladylike, agreeable, or the primary caretakers of children, it is incorrect to pigeonhole men into one-dimensional roles. Women are diverse in their interests and capabilities—and so are men. Yet these are the results of a patriarchal society. Men and boys *should* be able to be sensitive, cry, wear pink clothing, show fear, and dislike sports without risking ridicule or judgment.

Some practices and policies are designed to single out men in unfair ways. As a contingency plan, military conscription—also known as the draft—in the United States would only affect male civilians between the ages of eighteen and twenty-five; women couldn't be drafted.

While not as common or far reaching as sexism toward women, men certainly experience stereotyping in modern society in their own right. While this is not the same as systemic and institutionalized sexism, it has an

Magazine covers often present men as strong, athletic, professional, and successful. They, as well as women, are often featured for their physical appearance—with detrimental effects for consumers.

impact on the way society views and values men—and in turn, how women are treated.

ADDRESSING SEXISM

Confronting sexism in your own life begins with recognizing sexist comments and behaviors when you hear or see them. Some common forms of sexism that young women experience in school include:

- Interruptions from male students while female students or teachers are speaking;

- Modifications used to describe leadership roles for girls and women, as with adding the word "female" before a title—"female teacher" or "female student body president";
- Boys being called upon in class more often than girls; and
- Dress codes aimed at prohibiting specific clothing worn by female students without equivalent restrictions for male students.

If you have witnessed or experienced these or any other sexist situations, you may feel an urge to challenge people's ideas about gender roles. Some strategies you can use include:

Ask why: If a boy in class says or does something sexist, call them out by asking if they would treat a male friend the same way. You can call out their behavior in nonthreatening ways, even using humor, to make the point that girls shouldn't be treated differently than boys in your class.

Break gender-specific norms: If a girl is asked to do a traditionally female task, such as taking notes at a club meeting or ordering food for the group, she could challenge one of her male classmates to do it instead.

Take a stand: In instances where sexist comments are offensive or inappropriate, face the comments head-on. Simple, firm, but diplomatic statements such as "Please don't make those kinds of comments in my presence," can help address the issue without inciting confrontation or violence.

Speak to an adult: If you or someone you know finds themselves to be a constant target of sexist comments or actions, locate a trusted adult to confide in. This can be a parent or guardian, teacher, school counselor, principal, or even a friend's parent. Tell him or her who is saying these comments, when they are being said, and how they make you feel. Ask an adult to help you confront the student in a nonthreatening way or to help you find ways to avoid the student. A family or community member can also accompany you to speak to a teacher or school principal.

Many teens have part-time jobs and sometimes a supervisor or coworker is the one making sexist comments. If this happens, seek out another supervisor to speak with, talk to a trusted adult, or contact the company's human resources department to seek their advice or file a complaint.

When it's hostile, walk away: In cases where sexist comments or behavior have become aggressive, personal safety is more important than pointing the finger. If a person's comments or actions turn violent or threatening, or you simply do not feel safe in that person's presence, do *not* engage in an argument or physical confrontation. Seek a public place that is well-lit and well-populated. As soon as possible, call a parent or trusted adult and stay away from the person making threats. If the situation warrants it, you may need to call the police.

CHAPTER FOUR

SEXISM IN SOCIETY

I n September 2016, *Girls' Life* and *Boys' Life* magazines released their normal monthly issues. Each magazine had covers depicting widely divergent, and arguably sexist, content. The *Girls' Life* cover touted features titled "Wake up pretty," "Your dream hair," and "My first kiss." *The Boys' Life* cover highlighted a feature story titled "Explore Your Future: Astronaut? Artist? Firefighter? Chef? Here's how to be what you want to be."

Social media exploded. Many people called out the two different covers and their content as sexist and demeaning toward girls. Some asked why careers and college weren't the focus of the girls' magazine as well. Author and freelance writer Jennifer Wright tweeted a picture of the two covers side-by-side and sarcastically captioned them with the following comment: "Why are you feminists always complaining? We treat boys and girls exactly the same."

The cover differences between *Girls' Life* and *Boys' Life* are just an example of how people are fed information about gender roles and expectations in society at a very young age.

SEXISM BEGINS AT THE TOY STORE

Step inside almost any toy store, and it's easy to locate the toys marketed for girls—just head to the aisles plastered in pink and purple. Many girls' toys predominantly focus on the traditional gender roles of mother and homemaker. Kitchen sets and toy versions of household items like vacuum cleaners endorse the idea that these activities are things that girls and women do. By contrast, boys' toys encourage construction, science, discovery, and general learning. Or—one might argue—things that boys have "traditionally" done.

Toys divided by gender and gender roles teach children from very early ages that there are differences between girls and boys. While many little girls play with trains and trucks and many little boys play with dolls and kitchen sets, most of these toys are not marketed to be gender neutral. This lack of gender-neutral toys has not gone unnoticed.

In 2012, McKenna Pope, a New Jersey teenager, created a Change.org petition to encourage Hasbro, a prominent toy maker, to change the colors of its Easy-Bake Ultimate Oven. The oven was typically packaged in feminine colors like pink or purple. Pope, who was inspired by her younger brother's interest in cooking, wanted to get him the oven as a holiday gift, but found the colors too "girly." She was worried her brother would feel immediately discouraged from using the toy if she gave him one that was pink.

Her petition was signed by more than forty thousand people and gained the support of several male celebrity chefs, including Manuel Trevino of TV's *Top Chef*; Michael

The Easy-Bake Oven, marketed to young girls, came in gender-specific colors like purple and pink. Thanks to McKenna Pope, the toy is now offered in neutral colors appealing to young boys who want to explore the culinary arts.

Lomonaco, chef and owner of Porterhouse New York; and Bobby Flay, owner of Bar Americain and Mesa Grill, and the host of several cooking shows on the Food Network. Hasbro took notice and invited Pope to visit Hasbro and meet the team behind the Easy-Bake Oven. In 2013, Hasbro introduced a neutral-colored oven at the New York Toy Fair. The oven is now available in more neutral colors, including white, black, and silver.

THE PINK TAX: GENDER-BASED PRICING

Until the Affordable Care Act was passed, facilitating universal health care, it was legal for insurance companies to charge women more for the same health care coverage they provided to men. Sometimes, coverage could cost a woman 50 percent more. According to an article on the website Healthline.com, price differences occur because women are "higher risk" than men—they tend to visit the doctor more frequently, live longer, and give birth to children. The Affordable Care Act prohibited gender discrimination in health care insurance pricing.

Women and girls still pay more for other products as well. It's unofficially called the Pink Tax, and its name comes from the color of products marketed to girls and

The cost of being a woman is evident in grocery store aisles, where menstrual hygiene products are both expensive and taxed as nonessential items.

women. The Pink Tax is the price difference girls and women pay for products marketed specifically to them, versus gender-neutral products or goods marketed to men and boys. In many cases, the products are exactly the same—the only difference being color. Some examples include clothing, toys, and feminine hygiene products. On average, girls' clothing costs 4 percent more and women's clothing 8 percent more than boys' and men's clothing. Even identical items by the same manufacturer that differ only in color can be priced differently. Toys for girls cost approximately 7 percent more than toys for boys. Women's razors, shaving cream, and hair products all cost more than brands marketed to men. Women's products are even sold in smaller packages for higher prices, a practice manufacturers call "shrink it and pink it." Most shockingly of all, feminine hygiene products such as tampons are subject to sales tax in most states, while other medical necessities are tax exempt.

TITLE IX: CREATING EQUALITY FOR WOMEN

In 1972, Title IX of the Education Amendments Act of 1972 became a federal law, providing equal opportunities for women and girls in education and sports. Title IX states, "No person in the United States shall, on the basis of sex, be excluded from participation in, be denied the benefits of, or be subjected to discrimination under any education program or activity receiving federal financial assistance." As a result, Title IX has had a positive impact on women and girls at every level of athletic and educational participation, including:

- *Equal access to higher education*—Before the law passed, it was legal for colleges and universities to refuse to admit women.
- *Equality in career-related courses*—Prior to Title IX, many boys were automatically enrolled in shop and technology classes while girls were enrolled in home economics classes, with little to no cross enrollment. Title IX made it impossible for school administrators to order students to take certain classes based on gender.
- *Protection for pregnant students or students with children*—It was legal to expel students who were pregnant before Title IX was enacted. Now, schools may create programs for student-parents, but they must meet current school curriculum standards and enrollment must be optional.
- *Fighting sexual harassment*—Title IX requires schools to become legally obligated to prevent sexual harassment, and all incidents must be reported.
- *Increased access to athletics and athletic scholarships*—What may be the most widely recognized impact of Title IX is the increased access for girls and women to participate in sports. Title IX made it mandatory for schools and colleges to offer the same number of athletic teams for girls as it does for boys. Before Title IX, one in every twenty-seven high school girls played sports. By 2001, one in every 2.5 girls played sports.

SEXISM IN SPORTS

Athletics is one of the largest fields where gender inequality and sexism is still prevalent. From commentary that focuses more on female athletes' appearances instead of their performances to huge contrasts in pay between male and female professional athletes, equality for female athletes is lagging.

Of the top twenty-five highest paid athletes of 2016, not one woman makes the list. The highest paid female athlete of the year is tennis player Serena Williams, who has been ranked the number one female tennis player seven times in her career, and her total of twenty-three Grand Slam singles titles is a record for the most wins in the four major tennis tournaments by any tennis player, male or female. In 2016, Williams earned $28.9 million. By contrast, Cristiano Ronaldo, a Portuguese professional soccer player who plays for the Portugal national team and the Spanish professional club team Real Madrid, earned $88 million that same year.

OFF-THE-MARK COMMENTARY

During the 2016 Summer Olympic Games, the *Chicago Tribune* described trapshooting bronze medalist Corey Codgill as the "wife of a [Chicago] Bears lineman." The article failed to mention her by name and instead identified her by her marriage to her husband, a professional football player. While offering commentary on Katinka Hosszu, a record-breaking swimmer from Hungary, NBC's Dan Hicks talked about Hosszu's husband when he was shown in the stands and said,

"There's the guy responsible for turning Katinka Hosszu, his wife, into a whole different swimmer." While American swimmer Katie Ledecky was breaking the world record in the 400-meter freestyle, NBC's Rowdy Gaines made the following comment, "Some people say she swims like a man." Upon seeing Sanne Wevers, a gymnast for the Netherlands, writing in a notebook after completing her balance beam routine, NBC's Al Trautwig wondered if she was writing in her diary. Fellow commentator and 2008 Olympic gold medalist Nastia Liukin, also a commentator, corrected Trautwig, suggesting that Wevers was most likely calculating her scores.

EQUAL PAY FOR EQUAL PLAY

The US women's national soccer team has been fighting to be paid the same amount as the US men's national team. The men's team is paid almost four times as much in salary and bonuses as the women's team. And in cases where individual female players are paid the same as their male counterparts, it's not for equal amounts of playtime. In 2015, Hope Solo, the goalkeeper for the women's team, was paid approximately $366,000 by the US Soccer Federation, the official governing body for soccer in the United States. The organization oversees all amateur and professional soccer competitions, including the men's and women's national teams, and sets the salaries and bonuses for national team players. The year before, Tim Howard, the goalkeeper for the men's team, was paid $398,495. Solo's salary was for the twenty-three games she played that year; Howard's was for eight games.

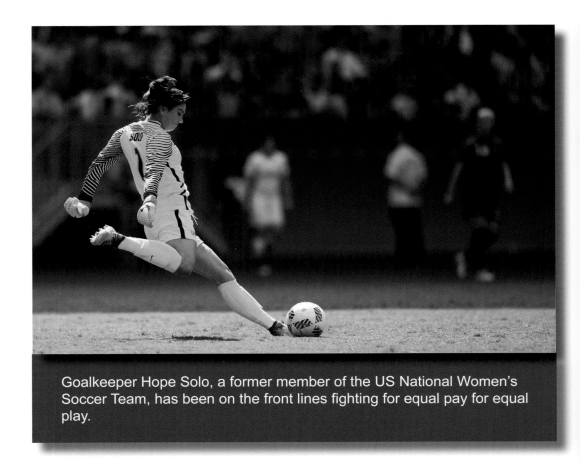

Goalkeeper Hope Solo, a former member of the US National Women's Soccer Team, has been on the front lines fighting for equal pay for equal play.

In addition, the women's team has been more successful in their victories and titles compared to the men's team. The women's team has won three World Cup championships and four Olympic gold medals. In 2015, more than 25.4 million people tuned in to watch the women's World Cup Final, a match that saw the US women's team beat Japan for the championship. It was the largest viewing audience ever in the United States for a soccer match. By contrast, the men's team has never won a World Cup and their highest-placed finish in the tournament was in 1930, when the team finished in third place. Their second-highest finish came in 2002 when the team finished eighth. The men's highest Olympic finish was eighth place in 1956. They have never won an Olympic medal.

According to the financial reports of the US Soccer Federation, the women's team brought in $20 million more in revenue over the men's team in 2015. As a result, the US women's team has filed a wage discrimination complaint against the US Soccer Federation asking for equal pay for equal play.

CHAPTER FIVE

LEADING THE FIGHT

Whether girls and women are standing up and demanding an unbiased dress code, equal treatment in classrooms, or equal pay for equal play on the professional sports field, confronting sexism and challenging sexist behaviors and viewpoints works for the betterment of society—regardless of gender.

ORGANIZATIONS FOR CHANGE

Confronting and changing the way women and girls are treated begins with the universal acceptance that sexism is a legitimate social issue that impacts everyone. Several national organizations are leading the fight to reduce and eliminate sexism and create a more equal environment for all.

THE NATIONAL ORGANIZATION FOR WOMEN (NOW)

NOW is a national organization that works to bring about equality for all women and girls. The organization focuses its efforts on a range of women's issues, including women's rights, economic justice, equal pay, racial discrimination, reproductive rights, family law, marriage and family rights for same-sex couples, and the positive representation of women and girls in the media.

NOW was founded in 1966. Its members—which included Betty Friedan, the author of *The Feminine Mystique*, and Shirley Chisholm, the first African American woman elected to the United States Congress—helped to write the legislation for women's rights that became part of the Civil Rights Act of 1964.

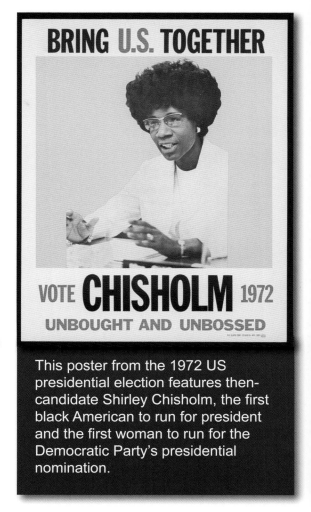

This poster from the 1972 US presidential election features then-candidate Shirley Chisholm, the first black American to run for president and the first woman to run for the Democratic Party's presidential nomination.

AMERICAN ASSOCIATION OF UNIVERSITY WOMEN

As one of the oldest organizations dedicated to equality for women, the American Association of University Women was founded in 1881 to counter a then-commonly believed myth that a college education would harm a woman's health and result in infertility. This myth was perpetuated by Dr. Edward H. Clarke, a Boston-based physician, and was debunked in the early 1900s.

Since then the organization's research has sought to educate and promote the education of and equal opportunity for women and girls.

GIRLS INC.

Girls Inc. was formed in 1864, in Waterbury, Connecticut. Originally the organization offered programs assisting working women and their daughters, who had nowhere to go when their parents were working. During the Great Depression, the group offered young girls a safe place to gather. Later, in the midst of World War II, when women filled jobs vacated by men who had gone off to war, Girls Inc. created educational programs for young girls whose mothers were working to support their families.

The organization has evolved to promote math and science education for girls, pregnancy and drug abuse prevention programs, increased media and economic literacy, adolescent health and violence prevention, and increased participation in sports. The organization also hosts a National Scholars Award, which recognizes outstanding Girls Inc. members with college scholarships.

#ASKHERMORE

Academy Award–winning actress Reese Witherspoon got sick of being asked about fashion on the red carpet while her male costars were questioned about their roles, political views, and other more thought-provoking questions. So, she decided to take on reporters herself by starting the #AskHerMore campaign.

Directed at journalists and the media, #AskHerMore was designed to prompt reporters to ask female actors, producers, and directors questions about their creative endeavors, the impact of film and television on society, and how filmmaking can take on social issues. "This is a movement to say we're more than our dresses," Witherspoon told Robin Roberts of ABC News during the network's Oscar preshow broadcast. Witherspoon,

Actress Reese Witherspoon, an Academy Award-winning actress and prolific producer, launched #askhermore, a campaign to engage actresses in more substantive conversations on the red carpet.

who was nominated for best actress at the 2015 Academy Awards, announced earlier that day that she would not reveal the designer of her gown until later in the evening. She posted on social media: "I love the Oscars AND fashion like many of you... But I'd also love to answer some of these Qs."

THE 2017 WOMEN'S MARCH

On Saturday, January 21, 2017, millions of women around the world gathered to protest on the first full day of President Donald Trump's tenure as the forty-fifth president of the United States. In cities large and small across all continents, women joined together to show their support of women's rights and equality—and to publicly protest the numerous sexist and demeaning comments Trump made about women during his election campaign. What began as a planned gathering in Washington, DC, our nation's capital and the location of

The Women's March on Washington, held on January 21, 2017, the day after President Donald J. Trump's inauguration, became a global event with millions of women joining marches and rallies around the world.

the White House, spread to include marches and rallies throughout the country and around the world.

Trump, who was inaugurated the day before the marches, made many inappropriate comments about women during his campaign. About Carly Fiorina, chief executive officer of Hewlett-Packard and a Republican candidate running against Trump during the primaries, Trump said: "Look at that face! … Would anyone vote for that? Can you imagine that, the face of our next president?" About Alicia Machado, a former Miss Universe, Trump said, "She was a winner, and she gained a massive amount of weight, and we had a real problem." In an interview with MSNBC's Chris Matthews, Trump commented, "There has to be some form of punishment" for women who get an abortion. Many women were angered by Trump's sexist rhetoric during campaign rallies, debates, and interviews. People were offended that Trump chose to suggest that women find alternate employment when faced with sexism in the workplace, verbally attacked women's appearances, and suggested retribution for their personal health care decisions.

It was estimated that more than five hundred thousand women were in attendance on the National Mall in Washington, DC. Similar gatherings occurred around the country in cities such as New York, Los Angeles, and Boston. In total, there were protests and rallies in 605 American cities. On the same day, around the world in cities including Sydney, Auckland, Paris, Rome, London, Bangkok, and Tokyo, women joined together to show their support and raise awareness for gender equality.

The marches were followed by work strikes in cities around the country. On Thursday, February 16, 2017, and on Wednesday, March 8, 2017, two work and spending strikes were organized in the United States. A Day Without Immigrants and A Day Without Women called upon immigrants and women to skip work and not spend money on these two dates as a way to demonstrate the economic strength and political clout of these demographics. As a result, women have shown higher interest in challenging sexist thinking and fighting for equality at the highest levels of local and national government. Training programs like California Women Lead, Emerge America, and Ready to Run have formed to help women launch political campaigns. Many of the programs, including Ready to Run, met their capacities for enrollment and are adding additional spaces to accommodate the increasing interest.

FUTURE OF SEXISM

In the last 100 years, women have fought for and earned the right to vote and the right to equal educational opportunities. They have helped write the legislation that made workplace discrimination illegal. In 2016, Hillary Clinton became the first woman backed by a major political party to run for president of the United States. But as significant as these accomplishments are, there is still much to be done to create an equal world for men and women. According to a Pew Research Center report in 2015, women earned 83 percent of what men earned.

You, too, can become a leader for change by educating yourself on sexism, learning positive strategies for confronting sexist comments and behaviors, and being persistent in seeking out and taking advantage of equal educational opportunities.

In 2016, Hillary Clinton became the first woman backed by a major political party to run for president of the United States. She showed strength during the presidential debates, unruffled by then-nominee of the Republican Party, Donald Trump.

Research suggests that as younger generations become more tolerant and inclusive of all people—including women, minorities, and members of the LGBTQ+ communities—sexism will become less pervasive. The more women and girls stay involved and keep fighting to raise awareness and demand equal treatment, the more widely gender inequality will become recognized as a universal social issue affecting everyone. And when it becomes everyone's problem, there is more likelihood for change.

10 GREAT QUESTIONS
TO ASK A GUIDANCE COUNSELOR

1. I would like to start a club on campus for young feminists. Where do I begin?

2. What are some other ways I can help educate people about sexism within our school's curriculum and programming?

3. I want to stand up to sexist behavior at school, but I am afraid of being bullied or becoming a target myself. What policies does this school have in place for reporting discrimination anonymously?

4. I hear male students making sexist comments about myself and/or my fellow students. How can I reach out to a teacher or staff member for help?

5. If I see a teacher or another authority figure acting in a sexist way, what steps can I take to confront that situation?

6. If I'm offered a part-time job after school, how can I find out if my hourly wage is the same as it is for male employees?

7. Is there such a thing as a "bad feminist"?

8. What are some effective strategies for expressing how sexist comments affect me on a personal level?

9. A friend of mine is making inappropriate comments. How do I decide if what he or she is saying is bad enough to risk compromising our friendship over?

10. My friend is dating someone with sexist beliefs. I'm worried she might get hurt. How and when is it OK for me to step in?

GLOSSARY

administrator A person who manages an organization, such as a school.

advocacy Actions taken in support of a belief or to support political issues.

amendment A change or alteration made to the US Constitution.

bias The personal judgment of others.

chauvinism The attitude that males are superior to females.

continuum A continuous series; range.

dependability Capable of being reliable, trustworthy, or consistent.

discrimination Perceiving a negative difference between groups of people.

femininity Qualities or traits traditionally associated with being female.

feminism The belief that men and women should have equal rights and opportunities.

gender The state of being male, female, or neither based on social rather than biological differences.

inequality Lack of sameness between groups of people.

masculinity Qualities or traits traditionally associated with being male.

objectify To degrade a person or see them as an object.

patriarchy Social and political structures in which men are the head of the family and/or the primary decision makers.

prejudice An adverse opinion or attitude created toward a group of people before having knowledge of the group.

prohibition An order to halt or stop; restraint.

stereotype A generalized opinion of an entire group of people that may often be untrue.

FOR MORE INFORMATION

Federated Women's Institutes of Canada (FWIC)
359 Blue Lake Road
PO Box 209
St. George, ON NOE 1N0
Canada
Website: http://fwic.ca
Facebook: @WomensInstitutes
Twitter: @FWICanada
Instagram: @FWICanada
Formed in 1919, representatives of provincial Women's
Institute (WI) groups met in Winnipeg, Manitoba, to
create the Federated Women's Institutes of Canada.
Today, the FWIC continues its long tradition of giving
voice to rural women and speaking out nationally on
behalf of women and families.

Girls Inc.
120 Wall Street
New York, NY 10005-3902
(212) 509-2000
Website: http://www.girlsinc.org
Twitter: @girls_inc
Instagram: @girlsinc
YouTube: @GirlsIncorporated
Girls Inc. is a national organization that seeks to help
educate girls on how to navigate gender, economic,
and social barriers so they can grow up to be
educated and independent young women.

Girls on the Run
801 East Morehead Street, Suite 201

Charlotte, NC 28202

(704) 376-9817

Website: https://www.girlsontherun.org

Facebook: @girls.on.the.run.international

Twitter: @gotri

Instagram: @girlsontheruninternational

YouTube: @girlsontherunint

Girls on the Run promotes positive emotional, social, mental, spiritual, and physical development in girls ages eight to thirteen years old. Through running programs and workouts, Girls on the Run aims to prevent girls from engaging in at-risk activities as the organization helps to build girls' self-esteem and self-worth.

National Council of Women of Canada (NCWC)

PO Box 67099

Ottawa, ON K2A 4E4

Canada

(909) 422-8485

Email: pres@ncwcanada.com

Website: http://www.ncwcanada.com

The National Council of Women of Canada (NCWC) works to improve conditions of life for women, families, and communities by empowering women to work together through a forum of member organizations and individuals. The NCWC was founded in 1893 and has been designated by the Canadian government as being of historical significance for its role in Canadian women's history.

National Women's Hall of Fame

76 Fall Street

PO Box 335

Seneca Falls, NY 13148

(315) 568-8060

Website: https://www.womenofthehall.org

Twitter: @WomenoftheHall

Instagram: @womenofthehall

The National Women's Hall of Fame is dedicated to honoring the achievements of American women. Located in Seneca Falls, New York, birthplace of the American Women's Rights Movement, the hall of fame offers events and programming to raise awareness of women's issues and celebrate the contributions of women to American society.

Native Women's Association of Canada (NWAC)

155 International Road, Unit #4

Akwesasne, ON K6H 5R7

Canada

1 (800) 461-4043 / (613) 722-3033

Website: https://www.nwac.ca

Twitter: @NWAC_CA

Instagram: @nwac_ca

The Native Women's Association of Canada (NWAC) works to advance the well-being of aboriginal women and girls, as well as their families and communities, through activism, policy analysis, and advocacy. NWAC is one of five officially recognized National Aboriginal Organizations (NAOs) whose purpose is to represent and speak, at the national level, on behalf of aboriginal women in Canada.

Women in Sport

26 Finsbury Square, 3rd Floor

London, UK EC2A 1DS

(020) 3137-6263
Website: https://www.womeninsport.org
Facebook: @ukwomeninsport
Twitter: @womeninsport_uk
Instagram: @womeinsport_uk
Women in Sport is an international organization promoting
    equality for women in sports. Through campaigns and
    partnerships, Women in Sport raises the visibility of
    female athletes, promotes the physical and mental
    benefits of exercise, and seeks to create equal
    opportunities for women and girls at all levels of play.

YWCA
National Headquarters
1020 19th Street NW, Suite 750
Washington, DC 20036
(202) 467-0801
Website: http://www.ywca.org
Twitter: @ywcausa
The Young Women's Christian Organization (YWCA) is
    dedicated to providing equal opportunities to women
    and girls by promoting equality and dignity for girls
    and women in communities around the country.

WEBSITES

Because of the changing nature of internet links, Rosen
Publishing has developed an online list of websites
related to the subject of this book. This site is updated
regularly. Please use this link to access this list:

http://www.rosenlinks.com/SPKUP/Sexism

FOR FURTHER READING

Abushanab Higgins, Nadia. *Feminism: Reinventing the F-Word.* Minneapolis, MN: Twenty-First Century Books, 2016.

Bennett, Jessica. *Feminist Fight Club: An Office Survival Manual for a Sexist Workplace.* New York, NY: Harper Wave, 2016.

DeMoss, Nancy Leigh, and Dannah K. Gresh. *Lies Young Women Believe: And the Truth that Sets Them Free.* Chicago, IL: Moody Publishers, 2008.

Fonda, Jane. *Being a Teen: Everything Teen Girls & Boys Should Know About Relationships, Sex, Love, Health, Identity & More.* New York, NY: Random House, 2014.

Ignotofsky, Rachel. *Women in Science: 50 Fearless Pioneers Who Changed the World.* New York, NY: Ten Speed Press/Crown Publishing, 2016.

Jenson, Kelly. *Here We Are: Feminism for the Real World.* Chapel Hill, NC: Algonquin Young Readers, 2017.

Sales, Nancy Jo. *American Girls: Social Media and the Secret Lives of Teenagers.* New York, NY: Vintage/ Knopf Publishing, 2016.

Schatz, Kate. *Rad Women Worldwide: Artists and Athletes, Pirates and Punks, and Other Revolutionaries Who Shaped History.* New York, NY: Ten Speed Press/ Crown Publishing, 2016.

Shetterly, Margot Lee. *Hidden Figures* (Young Readers' Edition). New York, NY: HarperCollins, 2016.

Stone, Tanya Lee. *Girl Rising: Changing the World One Girl at a Time.* New York, NY: Wendy Lamb Books/ Random House, 2017.

BIBLIOGRAPHY

Alter, Charlotte. "Reese Witherspoon Slams Sexist Red Carpet Questions, Encourages Journalists to #AskHerMore." Time.com, February 23, 2017. http://time.com/3718008/oscars-2015-askhermore-reese-witherspoon.

Bates, Laura. "10 Myths That Blame Women for Sexism." *Guardian*, August 7, 2014. https://www.theguardian.com/lifeandstyle/womens-blog/2014/aug/07/10-myths-that-blame-women-for-sexism.

Brown, Anna, and Eileen Patten. "The Narrowing, But Persistent, Gender Gap in Pay." Pewresearch.com, April 3, 2017. http://www.pewresearch.org/fact-tank/2017/04/03/gender-pay-gap-facts.

Chadband, Emma. "Nine Ways Title IX Has Helped Girls and Women in Education." NEAToday.com, June 21, 2012. http://neatoday.org/2012/06/21/nine-ways-title-ix-has-helped-girls-and-women-in-education-2.

Chemaly, Soraya. "All Teachers Should Be Trained to Overcome Their Hidden Biases." Time.com, February 13, 2015. http://time.com/3705454/teachers-biases-girls-education.

Cougar Hall, P., Joshua H. West, and Shane Hill. "Sexualization in Lyrics of Popular Music from 1959 to 2009: Implications for Sexuality Educators." *Sexuality & Culture*, Volume 16, Number 2, pp. 103–117 (June 2012).

Dasgupta, Nilanjana. "'Belonging' Can Help Keep Talented Female Students in STEM Classes." NSF.gov. Retrieved March 25, 2017. https://www.nsf.gov/discoveries/disc_summ.jsp?cntn_id=189603.

Fowler, Susan J. "Reflecting on One Very, Very Strange Year at Uber." February 19, 2017. https://www .susanjfowler.com/blog/2017/2/19/reflecting-on -one-very-strange-year-at-uber.

Goudreau, Jenna. "Is Chivalry Sexist?" Forbes.com, June 28, 2011. https://www.forbes.com/sites /jennagoudreau/2011/06/28/is-chivalry -sexist/#6d79f74c5ef5.

Grinberg, Emanuella. "Hasbro to Unveil Black and Silver Easy-Bake Oven after Teen's Petition." CNN.com, December 18, 2012. http://www.cnn.com/2012/12 /18/living/hasbro-easy-bake-oven.

Kaffer, Nancy. "Sexism Begins in the Toy Aisle." DailyBeast, November 30, 2014. http://www .thedailybeast.com/articles/2014/11/29/the-innate -sexism-of-christmas-toys.html.

Kohli, Sonali. "The Problem with Slut Shaming in Schools." *Los Angeles Times*, February 22, 2016. http://www.latimes.com/local/education/lausd /la-me-edu-slut-shaming-20160218-story.html.

Landsbaum, Claire. "Utah High-School Teacher Assigned 'Go on a Date' As Homework." *New York*, January 11, 2017. http://nymag.com/thecut/2017/01/utah-high -school-gave-students-sexist-date-assignment.html.

O'Donnell, Norah. "Team USA Members on Historic Fight for Equal Pay in Women's Soccer." CBS News, November 20, 2016. http://www.cbsnews.com /news/60-minutes-women-soccer-team-usa-gender -discrimination-equal-pay.

Pearson, Catherine. "16 Real Things Trump Has Said About Women While Running for President." Huffington Post, September 29, 2016. http://www .huffingtonpost.com/entry/16-real-things-trump-has

-said-about-women-while-for-running-for-president
_us_57e14a5ae4b04a1497b6a29c.

Plank, Elizabeth. "Robin Thicke's Sexism Isn't 'Blurry'."
Salon, July 28, 2013. http://www.salon.com/2013
/07/27/blurred_lines_is_clearly_sexist_partner.

Rimler, Rose. "Should Women Pay More for Healthcare
Services?" Healthline.com, June 13, 2016. http://
www.healthline.com/health-news/should-women-pay
-more-healthcare-services#1.

Shemkus, Sarah. "Rockport High School Leggings-Ban
Controversy Still Simmers." Boston Globe, March 6,
2014. http://www.bostonglobe.com/metro
/regionals/north/2014/03/06/rockport-high
-school-leggings-ban-controversy-still-simmers
/bB6p4Q7AQeriylACzAjlWJ/story.html.

Taylor, Susan Johnston. "The Pink Tax: Why Women's
Products Often Cost More." US News & World Report,
February 17, 2016. http://money.usnews.com
/money/personal-finance/articles/2016-02-17/the
-pink-tax-why-womens-products-often-cost-more.

Weiss, Suzannah. "7 Examples of Benevolent Sexism
That Are Just as Harmful as Hostile Sexism." Bustle
.com, December 23, 2015. https://www.bustle.com
/articles/131418-7-examples-of-benevolent-sexism
-that-are-just-as-harmful-as-hostile-sexism.

Zirin, Dave. "US Women's Soccer Is More Popular Than
Men's, But the Players Are Still Paid Less." Nation,
April 5, 2016. https://www.thenation.com/article
/us-womens-soccer-is-more-popular-than-mens-but
-the-players-are-still-paid-less.

INDEX

A

American Association of University Women, 45–46
#askhermore, 46–47

C

California Women Lead, 50
chauvinism, 13–14
Chisholm, Shirley, 45
Civil Rights Act of 1964, 14, 45
Clinton, Hillary, 50
Conway, Kellyanne, 28

D

Day Without Women, A, 50
double standards, 19, 20

E

education, sexism in, 4, 6, 22–23, 38–39, 45
Education Amendment Act of 1972, 38–39
Emerge America, 50
equal pay, 10, 13, 41, 43, 44

F

Feminine Mystique, The, 13, 45
feminism, 10, 13, 24, 34
Fowler, Susan, 8, 9–10
Friedan, Betty, 13, 45, 45

G

gender bias
    in education, 6, 18, 45
    in health care, 36–37
    in the media, 6, 29
gender discrimination, 14, 37, 39, 43
gender equality, 7, 10–12, 38–39, 49
gender norms, 32
gender stereotypes, 16, 25–26
Girls Inc., 46

H

head and master laws, 10–11
health care, sexism in, 36–37
Hollywood, sexism in, 6, 46–47
hostile sexism, 15, 16, 27, 33
human resources, 8

I

institutionalized sexism, 16, 30
internalized sexism, 16
interpersonal sexism, 16

L

lyrics, degrading, 22

M

misogyny, 13, 14
music, sexism in, 21–22

ABOUT THE AUTHOR

Laura La Bella is the author of more than forty nonfiction children's books. She has profiled actress and activist *Angelina Jolie: Goodwill Ambassador to the UN* (Celebrity Activists); reported on the declining availability of the world's fresh water supply in *Pollution, Drought, and Tainted Water Supplies* (Not Enough to Drink); and has examined the food industry in *Safety and the Food Supply*. La Bella lives in Rochester, New York, with her husband and two sons.

PHOTO CREDITS

Cover Aaron P. Bernstein/Getty Images; pp. 4–5 (background) igorstevanovic/Shutterstock.com; p. 5 Gregory Rec/Portland Press Herald/Getty Images; p. 6 Frederic J. Brown/AFP/Getty Images; pp. 8, 17, 25, 34, 44, 81/Shutterstock.com; p. 9 Justin Sullivan /Getty Images; pp. 11, 37, 47 © AP Images; p. 12 Bettmann /Getty Images; p. 18 DUEL/Cultura/Getty Images; p. 19 Chaideer Mahyuddin/AFP/Getty Images; p. 21 Paul Archuleta/FilmMagic /Getty Images; p. 23 Hulton Archive/Getty Images; p. 26 stock-eye/iStock/Thinkstock; p. 27 Ryan McVay/The Image Bank/ Getty Images; p. 29 Michael Loccisano/Getty Images; p. 31 Patti McConville/Alamy Stock Photo; p. 36 © Minneapolis Star Tribune/ZUMA Press Inc./Alamy Stock Photo; p. 42 Evaristo Sa/AFP/Getty Images; p. 45 Library of Congress Prints and Photographs Division; p. 48 Theo Wargo/Getty Images; p. 51 Saul Loeb/AFP/Getty Images.

Design: Michael Moy; Layout: Nicole Russo-Duca; Editor: Carolyn DeCarlo; Photo Research: Nicole DiMella